THE UNIVERSE

THE KUIPER BELT

ABDO
Publishing Company

A Buddy Book **by Fran Howard**

VISIT US AT

www.abdopublishing.com

Published by ABDO Publishing Company, 8000 West 78th Street, Edina, Minnesota 55439.

Printed in the United States.

Editor: Sarah Tieck
Contributing Editor: Michael P. Goecke
Graphic Design: Maria Hosley
Cover Image: Lushpix
Interior Images: Lushpix (page 11); NASA: (page 23, 27); NASA and Space Telescope Science Institute (page 5); NASA: Jet Propulsion Laboratory (page 13, 17, 21, 25, 30); Detlev van Ravenswaay / Photo Researchers, Inc. (page 9).

Library of Congress Cataloging-in-Publication Data

Howard, Fran, 1953-
  The Kuiper Belt / Fran Howard.
     p. cm. — (The universe)
  Includes index.
  ISBN 978-1-59928-927-4
  1. Kuiper Belt—Juvenile literature. 2. Solar system—Juvenile literature. I. Title.

QB695.H69 2008
523.48—dc22
                        2007027802

Table Of Contents

What Is The Kuiper Belt?

When people look up into the night sky, they can see the moon and the stars. Sometimes, they can even see planets glowing brightly.

There are also many objects that people can't see in the night sky. One of these is the Kuiper belt. It is at the far edge of our solar system.

So far, only the powerful *Hubble Space Telescope* has been able to capture images of the Kuiper belt.

Our Solar System

The Kuiper belt is part of our solar system. A solar system is a single star with many space objects, such as planets, orbiting it. Our sun is at the center of our solar system.

Earth is one of eight planets that orbit our sun. The other planets are Mercury, Venus, Mars, Jupiter, Saturn, Uranus, and Neptune.

Dwarf planets, comets, asteroids, and meteoroids also orbit our sun. And, scientists have discovered more than 100 moons in our solar system.

Our solar system

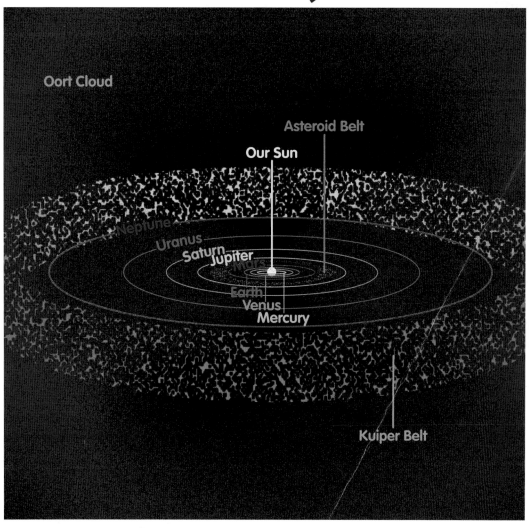

A Closer Look

The Kuiper belt is a cold, dark area of space. It lies beyond Neptune at the far edge of our solar system. Small space objects and the dwarf planet Pluto are found in the Kuiper belt. There, objects are made of frozen methane, ammonia, and water.

Objects in the Kuiper belt are mostly made of ice. They are smaller than planets. Most are between 6 and 30 miles (10 and 50 km) across.

In The Beginning

Scientists think that long ago, large planets were forming in the Kuiper belt. Some may have been as big as Earth!

However, Neptune was forming at this same time. Scientists think this planet's gravity caused objects in the Kuiper belt to **collide**. So, their growth stopped.

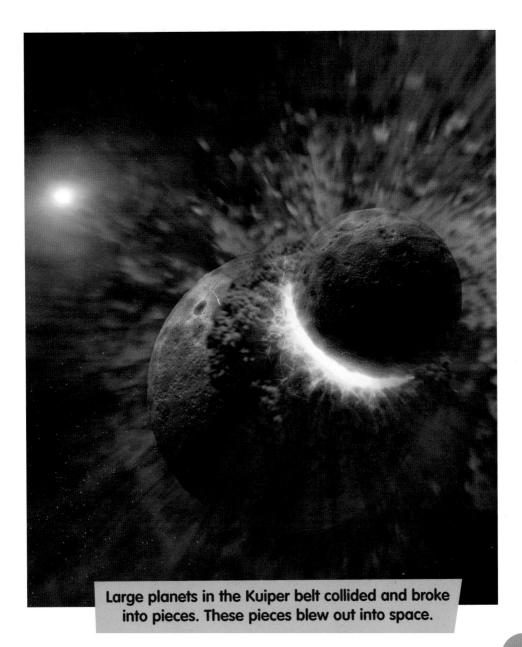

Large planets in the Kuiper belt collided and broke into pieces. These pieces blew out into space.

Kuiper Belt Objects

Kuiper belt objects are sometimes called KBOs. The dwarf planet Pluto was the first KBO to be discovered. Clyde Tombaugh discovered Pluto in 1930.

Charon

Pluto

Nix

Hydra

Pluto has three moons. Charon is the largest moon. It is about half the size of Pluto. Nix and Hydra (foreground) are much smaller.

13

The next KBO was not found until 1992. It is named 1992 QB$_1$. It is much dimmer and smaller than Pluto.

Scientists think that as many as ten KBOs could be nearly the size of Pluto. And there are small KBOs, such as comets.

Comets are round and icy, like giant snowballs in space.

Studying The Kuiper Belt

Over the years, scientists have discovered many KBOs. They have studied some of these. So, scientists know information, such as the sizes of several KBOs.

Pluto is one of the largest-known KBOs. Other large KBOs include Eris and 2005 FY_9.

Dysnomia

Eris

Eris is even larger than Pluto. A
moon called Dysnomia orbits Eris.

A KBO called 2003 EL_{61} is nicknamed Santa. Its surface is covered with frozen water. Also, Santa has two moons. They are called Rudolph and Blitzen.

Pluto's moon Charon is the fourth-brightest KBO. Some scientists say Charon may be another dwarf planet.

Orcus is another KBO. It is bigger than Charon. Scientists say it may also be a dwarf planet.

KBOs come in many different sizes and shapes.

Kuiper Belt Mysteries

There are still many mysteries about the Kuiper belt. For example, scientists are not entirely sure where KBOs formed. They think most formed in the Kuiper belt.

Also, some KBOs have disappeared over time. No one is sure why. Some scientists believe there were violent **collisions**, which destroyed them.

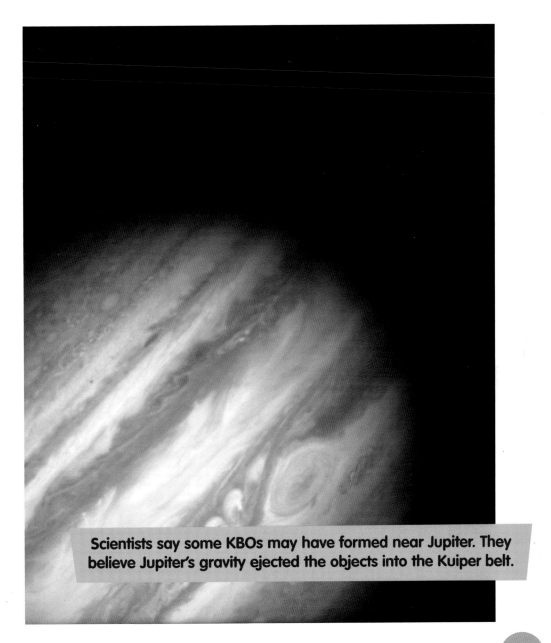

Scientists say some KBOs may have formed near Jupiter. They believe Jupiter's gravity ejected the objects into the Kuiper belt.

Kuiper Belt Discoveries

For many years, no one knew for sure if the Kuiper belt was real. In the 1940s, astronomer Kenneth Edgeworth wrote about the parts of the solar system beyond Neptune.

And in the 1950s, Gerard Kuiper discussed his own ideas about this part of space. Edgeworth and Kuiper were the first to say that the belt exists.

Gerard Kuiper was known for having very good eyesight. He claimed he could see stars that were too dim for most people to see.

In the mid-1900s, telescopes weren't strong enough to see beyond the farthest planets. And, KBOs are not very bright. Still, several scientists came to believe the Kuiper belt existed.

In the 1990s, astronomers spotted several KBOs. This helped them prove the Kuiper belt exists.

Scientists still have many questions about the Kuiper belt and KBOs. They are searching for new information to help them learn more.

Astronomers David Jewitt and Jane Luu located some KBOs in 1992. They used telescopes at the Keck Observatory in Hawaii.

Visiting The Kuiper Belt

So far, no **spacecraft** has visited the Kuiper belt. To learn more, scientists have used powerful telescopes. Some are located in space. Others are on Earth.

The first spacecraft to fly into the Kuiper belt will be *New Horizons*. The United States **launched** this **mission** on January 19, 2006. *New Horizons* is the fastest spacecraft ever launched. It can travel 36,000 miles (58,000 km) per hour!

New Horizons is about the size of a piano. It was sent into space aboard an *Atlas V* rocket.

Fact Trek

For many years, scientists said Pluto was the ninth planet. But now, it is considered a dwarf planet. Many scientists are still discussing this!

It takes 248 Earth years for Pluto and Charon to orbit the sun.

Pluto's orbit is irregular. It follows an egg-shaped pattern.

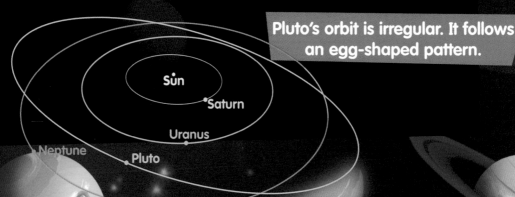

Sun

Saturn

Uranus

Neptune

Pluto

In space, distance is measured in light-years and light-minutes. One light-year is how far light would travel in one year. Light travels nearly 6 trillion miles (10 trillion km) in a year!

Think about how fast light fills a room when you flip a switch!

The sun is the closest star to Earth. It is eight light-minutes away. Proxima Centauri is the second-closest star to Earth. It is about four light-years away.

Proxima Centauri is part of a constellation, or group of stars, called Centaurus.